Changeling Studios

Propoganda Poete

OsoLobo

Being the chronicles of a
poet's journey whilst trying to
survive and process this epic
amount of global trauma.

This one is for me,
Because I simply HAD to do it.
(Hopefully I will leave this place at least a little
better than I found it...)

Shout out to Noelia Cerna for inspiring me
with the phrase Word Tornadoes!!

Part I:
Stormfront Horizons

The first rule of intelligent tinkering
Is to save all the pieces.
~Aldo Leopold~

Poetry is Suicide Prevention

In lieu of all
We are denied
Stripping away our humanity

At least we still have poetry

Inner Child Extroverted

Were it a color
My childhood would be blue
A dark pretty bruise

Poet Rising
(for Jennifer Gordon)

There once was a heart
That stood stories tall
Hard did it shatter
When it had a great fall
But after it broke
Something awoke
Now beautiful poetry
She shares with us all

Inklings

Paying for beauty
With pain
It's what we do

We are all tattooed

Dead Giveaway

Our souls tell stories
About the lies that hide
In our hearts

To Be Honest

I have secrets & so do you
T'is the one thing between us
We can be certain is true

Hopeless Romantic

Whenever I feel you near
I forget
The true nature of fire
Is to always consume

Complex

If I had a hammer
I would throw it like Thor
I would throw it to the farthest reaches
Of the Earth
And it would come back to me

If I had a hammer
I'd probably lose the damn thing
Just another silly little man
Trying to play God

"Labor Shortage"

nine lives lost to the cost of living
eight days a workweek never done
seven times survival screams
six souls cannot be saved
five more left alive
four bodies found
three ran down
two left
one…

Divided We Fall
(An American Haiku)

Freedom isn't free
That is the whole fucking point
Of masks and vaccines

Eat the Rich, Kill the Poor

Like a hunter hiding poison
In a piece of meat
So the prey will foolishly
Eat it
America delivers
Predatory capitalism
Dressed in democracy

Ode to America

Crescent moon
Reminds me of you
A sliver of hope
Disappearing into darkness

Immortal Mortality

Before:
T'is in the age
When birthdays become a
countdown
instead of a count up
One must recognize that
Forever
May not be quite as long
As perpetually advertised

After:
We're all just boneyard body bags
Wandering to and fro
Caging concealed spirits
Wondering when we'll let them go

Forever Moments

Lips on skin we invent sin
Our whispers waltz within the wind
We sly the sky the stars go shy
The moon so soon cries

Try

Try to hide what dreams inside
Pretend we fear this ride
To excite the flight
We'll steal sun's light
And let what may decide

Red Flags at Night

Your kisses may be poison
But as I lie here dying
I can see music
And hear colors

Halloween Love Poem

Trick or Treat
You're So Sweet
But I Have Diabetes

Loving you is like eating
Deep fried Twinkies
Slowly hardening my arteries
And seizing my heart

Genie What?

Isn't expecting forever
Kind of like wishing
For more wishes

Seasonal Affective Disorder

When everything dead
Outside
Reminds me of everything
Dead inside

In Lieu of True Leadership

The desire
To be an apex predator
Does not an alpha male make

Un(En)Titled

I wanted to write a poem
But I couldn't find a metaphor
More apropos than modern day Neros
Looking down on us
From space
Just watching
As the entire world burns

Ego Estranged

It's always me first
Until it comes time to be
Held accountable

Patriotic Christian Family
(A Found Poem)

No handouts, America
Get a job
Find Jesus

Jesus Still Weeps

Invoking Jesus
While denying human rights
What would Jesus do

Focus Groups

The active practice
Of fooling the sheep
Into doing the wolves' work
For them

Pawns Propagating Propaganda

If you accuse them of rioting
Without hearing their cries
Only harp on what's what
Never questioning the whys
Your train of thought has derailed
Your America has failed
When Black Lives Matter
Less than white lies

Say It With PRIDE!

My pronoun? That one
Dude who just kicked your ass you
Disrespectful fuck

LoveCats

furry overlord
brushes past in nonchalance
the distance of love

this beauty begs not
it shall never be conquered
 i still feel your smile

Collateral Damage

I used to wear my traumas
Like war paint
Until I realized
People just took that
As a challenge

Spoken Word Poetry
Online Open Mics
Saved My Life

Every time I spill my sunshine
You bring flowers to my darkness

In a world
That is far too ugly
Far too often
Your beauty keeps me
Alive

Sound the Alarm!

(Forgive the Interruption)

Haunted Valentine
(It's Word Tornado Season)

PROLOGUE (collab w/Zephrine MoonGarden):

She was sitting. Alone,
Raspberry Violet eyelashes and all....
Sharp breaths tinted in Crimson
escaping her lips...
actively extroverting to calm the Static inside,
(you have no idea...)

Sunset Dyed Horizon,
foreshadowed by the Chromatically Declined...
trying desperately not to wash it all Gray,
(because if it's a Gray day then nothing moves today)

Just like the space between Now and Hope,
(or the distance between Hope and Hopelessness...)

ACT I:
When outside looks like
An IG filter
Our reality shows
Its true nature
Even should it rain today,
not everyone complains.

ACT II:
Why must we cloud
Our sunshine
Just so we can
Throw our shade

ACT III:
There is a perverse poetry
In all the ways
You slowly kill me

Trying to work out what it's about
And why someone had to leave
~Elton John (And the Tide Will Turn...)~

Part II:

Residing in the Eye

We starve all the teachers and recruit more marines
How come we don't even know what that means?
~Joe Jackson (Obvious Song)~

Inclined to Be Incomplete

Lost in place
Lost in my own space
Losing grace
Losing my own face
Lonely race
Running my own pace
Leave no trace
Just another cold case
Lost in place
Lost in this empty space

When all the pain comes crushing in
The darkness longs to wear me thin
I fail the call to look within
Where answers...

<u>*A Poet's Journey*</u>

alone all along
forest morning still and calm
this journey begins

travel companions
make no sound in early hours
i find empty husks

words escape me now
i may have to hunt them down
blissful sleep beckons

inviting ground waits
i should lie down and look up
let the words find me

Ode to the Storm Gods
(For Elemen2al & Paul ConQueso)

you always strike twice
you are thunder and lightning
answering the call

we raindance in awe
raw power crashes the sky
inspiration calls

baptized by music
communing with poetry
these are my churches

Bridging the Gap
(Ever Onward)

there i was again
wondering where i was then
knowing now is gone

another long sigh
another long goodbye for
lessons of my youth

as truth burns my soul
i want to once again know
the joy of unknown

goodbyes are only
hellos dressed in the darkness
of our own demise

if we were not wise
we would address our goodbyes
and send them packing

leaving us lacking
the necessary skills for
that great leap forward

Holy Man with a Righteous Plan

the pagan world gone
new age holy daze feast up
on this old-world corpse

when blue flames play games
weaving through neuropathways
brain can trick the soul

the spiritual calls
spirituality falls
icons prey upon

can you find your way
if you allow others to
say which god to pray

<u>*Eye Spy*</u>

i know you see me
your camera eyes try to hide
i find you lacking

voyeuristic schemes
have no power over me
watch me all you want

you'll see me live life
living it on my own terms
watch me if you dare

<u>*My Blood Can't Breathe*</u>

just kiss me softly
Death, I prefer the slow dance
let us just begin

blue veins leave dark stains
your words become sticks and stones
bones fold into leaves

blood vessels tattered
branches reach for sustenance
mosaic pathways

the answer awaits
encircled circumstances
kaleidoscope views

barren white alone
attic-grown hiding spaces
never out of place

versed in performance
you play your part quite well dear
you always fooled me

across this archway
where two became one elsewhere
i lost myself there

afar is too far
distance spans towards happenstance
anxious fears steer clear

"books were safer than
other people anyway"
Neil Gaiman knew

Apart Together/Together Apart

When we were apart
I could still feel your heartbeat
Nerve endings pining

Supply and demand
The commodity of touch
Hiding in plain sight

Eye contact is rare
moments of separation
breed isolation

It doesn't seem right
We fight to remain unseen
Unless we're on screen

Apart together
Will the heart still remember
Together apart

Personal Effects Personal Affects

A house now vacant
Walls and halls still echoing
Personal effects

Space may be vacant
Spirits still retain your shapes
Personal affects

Soul's gone wandering
Shadows anchor darkness felt
Personal effects

Creeping into cracks
Pain attempts to take control
Personal affects

Personal effects
Linger in the folded fear
Personal affects

<u>*Shadow Boxed*</u>

angels dejected
their shadows spoke silent hues
painting hard questions

why blindly follow
ignoring nature within
disguise it with sin

self-abuse reflex
this is the true fall from grace
denial of self

better to rise up
divine in your own beauty
light up their darkness

better to rise up
divine in your own beauty
enlighten darkness

<u>*This New Earth*</u>

feet find gravel flaws
soles would seriously singe
this surface now stings

Odin's eye aside
rainbow bridges paint the sky
ravens watch the night

i want to live there
where the air is crisp and clean
where cliffs kiss the clouds

<u>*Unmarked No More*</u>

try to disguise lies
whitewashed history denies
oral traditions

native children now
rise again to remind us
past crimes are still here

remains revealed
built upon these buried truths
don't let them forget

little ones cry out
try to keep our past buried
spirits still shall rise

little ones call out
try to keep our past buried
our ghosts still shall dance

<u>*Necessary Renovations*</u>
(Mainlining Capitalism)

skyscraper storefront
bruises the clouds violet dark
corporate needles rain

sunrise door beckons
find your way to a new day
just step right on up

white privilege door slams
opportunity knocks not
remember your place

sunset door still looms
what rooms may wait we wonder
weaknesses abound

foundations crumble
frames falter under pressure
these cards *will* collapse

atop your tower
you fine dine on the skyline
your water shall fall

spill over the edge
trickle down to streets below
fuel the fire

this smoldering steam
shall someday scorch your vision
blinded to the truth

<u>*Drawing Borderlines in a Sandbox*</u>

Immigrant tears fall
Watering tomorrow's seeds
Hope blooms the children

The sands of sorrow
Shatters of glass tomorrow
Dreamers awaken

Fools' gold lies beneath
Where false prophesies bequeath
Hollow of promise

Taking toll breaking
Sandlines find the fissure faults
This box soon shall burst

The ashes of these dreams deterred
Rise again in voices yet unheard

<u>*Soul Capsule Unearthed*</u>
(A Self-Portrait)

the mirror holds tests
pass or fail matters not here
reflections hold still

on the precipice
looking towards the bitter seas
the truth in disguise

horizon storms rage
nature's lessons crash the shores
undertow awaits

when answers ask more
questions fill with gravity
what lies beneath lies

shedding the old ways
the barricades from within
once again begin

i buried you here
why are you rising anew
i do not want you

this haunting won't end
you pretend to be my friend
reopening wounds

you rise all too soon
failing to recognize signs
I resist once more

may i someday sense
this resurgence and rebirth
keep calling me out

listen, just be still
waters reflect energy
teach lessons of calm

take a deeper breath
the gut punch that never came
you can't punch puddles

Light bends defiant
speeds around in flashes warped
finding its own path

standing tall again
impact never comes this time
further tricked by light

darkness walks steady
absent of chosen pathways
mysteries abound

please send up the flares
downward spiral drills deeper
it is dark again

this introspection
inception spins round and round
losing my bearings

it may take longer
to walk around dark towers...
i can still see stars

Beware Rose Colors

barriers are just
glass panes we use to view life
through glass-pained lenses

we create senses
to make sense of self, framed by
lives we may have lost

choose wisely my friend
too much pretend only yields
shatters of stained glass

<u>Chrysalis</u>

sing me butterfly
your wings take me far away
dream of better days

sing me butterfly
your colors vivid in praise
of a better life

sing me butterfly
in your metamorphosis
you enlighten me

on butterfly wings
i shall fly again towards you
majesty of new

Part III:

Living in the Aftermath

*We're not here to take part,
We're here to take over
~Hed PE (Pay Me!)~*

LifeSpace
(for Naomi Shihab Nye, Kai Coggin &
The Summer Poetry Teachers Institute at The Poetry Foundation)

I woke up from a dream
And here there was
a poem
But what does it all mean?

Slow
        Us
                Down

Love
The mystery
Don't fear it

It's ok to daydream
In drops of rain
And daydrink
Beams of sun

One simple idea
Spreads
Into a kaleidoscope of spontaneous thought

Trust that moment

Momentarily mentioning
The intriguing
Infinity

Celebrate the birth
Of that first spirit
Writing poems to open up
Words
Without worrying about
What they all mean

I've never been anywhere
Where poetry doesn't want
To live
More

Leave it moving in the air
Growth and evolution
Doesn't explain itself
Make love to the magic
Add to the mystery
Revel in the ritual
Of sharing
The secrets
Worry not
About understanding it all

Allow the whys of wonder
To paint themselves
Outside the lines
Time and place need no face
Let imagination keep the pace

Don't pretend that people don't
Often tend
To just suture lines together
Attempting to outline forever
Art and life do not imitate
Imitation suggests limitation

Art and life are mirrors
Of endless reflection
We the poets must paint experience
Illustrating the lines we're living

Let the language linger
Let the feelings keep you reeling
For meaning
Means
Far
Less
Without feeling

So what does it all mean?

It means we need write
Like we mean it

<u>*Sixth Sense for Bullshit*</u>

I once heard a superhero say

"I can see seedy sheisters in a single glance
And leave them no chance
As I inhale the clouds
And breathe lightning"
       ~la Bruja

Then did I realize
I cannot change the skies
By questioning why
But I may be able to find a new way
Of playing with the sun

Beam some bright
Directly into this fight

Resist the gravity
Weighing down our reality
Imploding the elements
Within ourselves
Aiming to elevate
Our innerpowers to contemplate

So perhaps we shall not hesitate
Humanizing each other
Instead of villainizing the other
Innervisions of inner peace
Bringing wisdom
To our decisions

La Bruja Lightning once again exhaled in storms

"If we could just
Learn to love ourselves
to the level of who we are
Love ourselves
Like we should love our own children"

<u>Yeshwa</u>
(Black Jesus Matters)

They will hate you for the color of your skin

                    I shall love them anyway

They will despise you because you are kind

                    I shall help them anyway

They will covet your crown and take it from you

                    I shall give it to them anyway

They will hunger only for your power

                    I shall feed them anyway

They will use your truths to blind the world

                    I shall open their eyes anyway

They will kill you for speaking out against them

                    I shall live for them anyway

Bait and Switch

I really want to write a poem
To show em that it really is time
To put down the fucking guns
And stop slaughtering everyone

To reach enough people
To teach this hypocrisy dichotomy
Of being both pro-life and anti-gun control

For real Yo
This shit is taking its toll

But honestly, I just can't anymore

I really want to write a song
Where we all actually get along
And can rationally discuss
This Handmaid's Tale reality
Created by a GOP calamity
As they continue to use your own religion
As ammunition against you
To somehow spread contagion
Diametrically opposing
The actual teachings of your Christ

But honestly, I just can't anymore

I really want to write a story
Without all the gory details
About systematic oppression
Hiding racism's true intentions
I mean how many times do we have to learn
The same damn lessons
Before they actually leave an impression
And revolution finally gets more
Than just an honorable mention

But honestly, I just can't anymore

My America doesn't torture
My America doesn't kill

This bumper sticker wisdom
Might call out this system
That feeds upon the victims
But the problem still thrives

We do not live in the same America

It's us versus them
And we're at it once again
Divisive to the end
Yet still all struggling to survive

We do not live in the same America

This keeps us all apart
Separates us from our hearts
Stripping humanity from the start
Leaving us lost in all the cracks

We do not live in the same America

If we keep this status quo
We'll have nowhere left to go
With no potential room to grow
Leaving us all open to attack

Because we do
In fact
All live in the same America

These Sideshow Attractions
House Deeper Distractions

I am a manbun on a bald dude
Yeah I know, that shit don't make no sense
Well you're shit don't make no sense to me
All these false allegations of beauty
Like gallows poles throughout the centuries
Don't act like trending is a new thing
When popularity has been singing the praises
Of the master races
since the early phases of civilization

now if only there were more civility
in this citizenry
then maybe we could meet
at the cross-sections
of intersectionality
where dreams can dance with reality
and maybe
just maybe
instead of just coexisting
in this insanity
we could stop limiting
the definitions of humanity

Seeing Beauty in Person

If beauty were a person
She would exist within infernos
The fiery passions of volcanic flows
Scorching the skies of Mercury

If beauty were a person
She would be clouded in mystery
A necessary protection from predators
Who seek to prey upon her
Inner Venus heat

If beauty were a person
She would soar aloft
As free as falcon flights
Adrift on endless wind currents
Caressing the clouds of Earth

If beauty were a person
She would walk statuesque
Solid mountain giant
Across vast moonscapes and valleys
Rivaling those of Mars

If beauty were a person
She would loom larger than all
Draped in gaseous forms that keep her
Veiled from the naked eye
Released only in storms that ravage
Jupiter's hidden landscape

If beauty were a person
She would never have need
For the rings of men
Her radiance would overcome their gravity
Encircling the entirety of any Saturn

If beauty were a person
Her orbits would criss and cross
Without any type of loss
Gaining only the courage and certainty
Of the planetary twins, Uranus and Neptune

If beauty were a person
There would be no debate
Frigid frozen fears would be dwarfed
By her ability to be seen
No matter what any others may deem
What she should be
Planetary, plutonic or not
It is her decision
Not yours

If beauty were a person
She would Sol-shine so brightly
That all other versions
Would orbit around her
The center of all light and energy
Given freely
So that all things could live in harmony

If beauty were a person
She would be you
And you
And you
One continuously spiraling celestial spirit
An entire solar system
Of passions
Mystery
Freedom
Vast expanse
Ravaging storms
Radiance
And courage
Deftly defying any definitions of men

Ain't No Such Thing as a Favorite Book

(dedicated to Advocate of Wordz, Kai Coggin,
the whole Nuyorican Poets Café Online and WPN Poetry Families)

The first book I ever read
Was _Charlotte's Web_
And it taught me more about love and acceptance
Than the American School Indoctrination Systems ever could
And the _Incredible Hulk_ encouraged me not to sulk
But to rage, rage, rage
Before I even knew my light was dying
Judy Blume taught me not to assume
That a _Fourth Grade Nothing_
Would never find the courage to become something
The Giver gave me more than this world could ever take
By illustrating just how much of a mistake
It would be to live without poetry, music & art

And that was all before I really started this journey

In junior high
Stephen King and I became a daily thing
While everyone else was talking about rings and lords
The Gunslinger took me on a true hero's journey

He knew that he was meant to lose
But still he would choose
The Drawing of the Three
So he could travel through _Wastelands_
And continually risk everyone's ass
Just to find
Wizard and Glass

Until I read _The Crow_
I didn't know what true love truly was
My high school years
Brought plenty of tears
But it all turned out alright
As Mike Grell showed me _Green Lantern's Light_
And with every Green Arrow

That the *Longbow Hunters* shot
I knew that someday I would have my own shot
At making something in this world right again

Like a Super Soldier
I discovered the real *Truth*
When *Black Lightning* fought
The powers that be
And *The Falcon* was always
More than just a token sidekick
To me

But my eyes were truly opened
In my senior year
That was before Civics Class
Became a GOP Fear
When I had a teacher that truly
Inspired me
To inspire others

When One Flew Over the Cuckoo's Nest
I immediately thought that was the best
But then the *Tao of Pooh*
Helped me to figure out what to do
The Jungle and *Animal Farm*
Really made me **feel**
Why I should do no harm
And I was shown our true fate with
A People's History of the United States
Miseducation of the Negro
Showed me how this system has got to go!!
And I will never forget
The ultimate regret when
Johnny Got His Gun

A break from structured education
Took me to places beyond description
Where I met *Nine Princes in Amber*
Which of course led me
To *A Game of Thrones*
But after having to wade through

A *Storm of Swords* just to
Dance with Dragons
I had to move on to something a bit more
Substantial

Then Garth Ennis showed me
The depths of religion
As *The Preacher* went on a quest
To make God accountable for this mess
And the *Chronicles of Wormwood*
Would suggest
That Christianity was really
Just the Devil's Jest
And while that's all well and good
In a fictitious sense
It wasn't until Biblical Scholar Bart Ehrman
Turned Agnostic
By his own research
That I saw just how wrongly they were
Misquoting Jesus
And *Holy Blood, Holy Grail*
Revealed the actual historical tales
That led to *Davinci's Code*
But it was the unlikely tale
Of Scott Douglas that showed me
That we are all
God's Debris

In college I was fortunate enough
To find true knowledge
(no really
I know that's hard to believe)
Because of teachers
Who were actually there to teach
There were many important lessons
I received

A Handmaid's Tale
Gave a veiled warning
About a future we might just be
Living today

I was brought to *Shaman's Tears*
Because *Black Elk Speaks*
And a *Noble Red Man*
Gave me spiritual lessons to keep
When I spent *A Summer of Black Widows*
Watching *The Lone Ranger and Tonto Fistfight in Heaven*

Red Earth, White Lies really opened my eyes
To just how far the system will go
To falsely prove its own lies
Bury My Heart at Wounded Knee had a lot more to teach me
About the past being
More than just a warning

Recently
I took a motorcycle poetry roadshow journey
With 2000 miles of **Cauldrons**
Every day a new incantation
With a magical mixture of poetry potions
Cultivated by K.R. Morrison

And I still have yet to choose
Where to start **Mining for Stardust**
Incandescent, **Wingspan**,
Or a **Periscope Heart**
Perhaps I should listen to the sounds
Of **Silhouette**
It's like literary roulette
That I can never lose
When Kai Coggin's poetry
Is my sister muse

Without a doubt
I have to shout out
Gimme Timothy Moore
More more
Of dem **Urban Thoughts**
To open up all our blind Third Eyes
Speaking of Moore
B. Sharise I promise to give you a holla
As soon as I read **Dr. Marvellus Djinn's Odd Scholars**

So as you can see
Choosing a favorite
Would be hella difficult to conceive

Like the ***Ebb & Flow*** of Miro
I still have so many books to read

I mean
I have yet to have
Conversations with Grief
Loveletters to Gaia
I'm sure will just be full of fiyaa!
I'm certain ***Black Calculus*** will show me
Equations that lead to
Light Shadow Life
And I still need to see the joy
That can be found by a
Disappearing Boy
When I travel to
Three Mile Harbor
It'll probably help me see
Just how much this is all
Calamity
And I cannot wait to rage with Jane
And speak ***Words Against the Machine***

See what I mean?!?!
How can I choose a favorite book
When I still need to look
To all of you in this community
Artists, writers, poets, dancers, musicians, filmmakers, actors
I can never thank you all enough
For giving me these adventures
And showing me where to go
Even beyond the titles that I already know
There is still so much left to grow

Mad respect to all of you
For helping me to do so

Will the Real Higher Education Please Stand Up

They're hoarding knowledge in college
And selling it to the highest bidder
This is the bitter truth
Cutting off the youth
To any possibility of doing anything
Other than
Just scraping to survive
Preventing the possibility
Of actually living until they die

This is all by design
The system is full of it
All these red flags that say
If you don't play our way
Then good luck
Ever having a say
In how this all goes down...
The drain

I grow ever so tired
Of trying to explain
How this pain is created
The Architects' insatiable need
To feed all seven of their own deadly sins
Can never be sated
With all the hatred
That they created
While they scream about it all
Just being fake
Or trying to convince us all
That it's just innate
That we're all just ingrates
Who don't know how to appreciate

Well I'm here to thank you all
My global poetry family
For showing me that it's never too late

We can unlock all the knowledge we want
And it can all be for free
They don't have the only key
Street knowledge and Spoken Word College
Are always in session
Where we can learn the most important lessons
In our collective poetry slam sessions
Where we can manifest all the best inventions
With very real intentions
Of teaching and learning from each other
Each and every sister, each and every brother
So that maybe we can finally find a way
To fix all this shit
And maybe even move forward
Together

<u>*The Seasons of our Souls*</u>

Be like water
Go with the flow
Adapt
You can't punch puddles

But water can boil over
Singe the skin from within
Until life becomes
Unbearable

Water can freeze solid
To the point that it won't
Be moved
Lest movement and motion
Become danger and destruction
The devastating wake
Of glaciers grown wild
Melting away millions of miles

Water may be able to weather the storm
But the weather that water creates
Can bring devastation
Erode away at creation
As the waves crash away at the shores
Until it becomes impossible to ignore

Be like water
Go with the flow
Adapt
You can't punch puddles

But they can most certainly punch you

So stand like trees
Feel the breeze in your hair
As it leaves a trail on the wind
Breathing from within

To bring voice to the choices that need
To be

Ancestors freely roam in your soul
To grow
Seek the sky by asking why
Feel the reasons we deny
Standing like the trees

But how can leaves breathe
When the very air deceives
Our needs

Our roots contract in a desperate act
Like a gut punch
Drains the will to perceive

Can we answer back
This branch attack
Or leave our lungs
To erode into toxic cracks
That crater through
Our very attempts
To take a moment
And just breathe…

Ok, breaktime is over!

No more waiting for the smoke to clear
It's time to breathe fire
In arrears
Make up for so many lost years
These fears have taken up too much space
This scorched earth is no resting place
Phoenix fires still leave layers of ash
So where can we grow from here

Anger and passion may be in fashion
But lasting growth only comes from evolution
So the spirit must be willing to navigate real revolution
And true retribution

So yers!
Be like water
Stand like trees
Breathe in deep
Blaze higher degrees
Encourage the spirits to fly out free
How else will we ever get to where we need to be

Ripples
(Dedicated to all my sinner poets & proud weirdos!)

Let they who live *within* sin
Cast the first stone

Because we are not alone
This stone is
Skipping across the universe
Sending ripples like gravitational waves
That pave the ways
For creative forces to flow

Far better than just rolling the bones
These stone-thrown ripples
Always beat the house

Never to be taken for granted
These granite salutations
Create the foundations
That can bring down this Goliath nation
Of egofucktowers built on
Funeral wreath flowers
Reminding us that we have the power
If we just choose to live it

So don't tell us not to throw our stones
Just because you need to atone
For all of your sins against our humanity
That is the true profanity
Trying to pull it all apart
Instead of bringing us all together

Let us flock like birds
So we can spread the word
We must not let them cull our herd
With false prophesy
And forced autocracy
They will not block our way
We will have our say

It's time for us to have ourselves
A Real Judgement Day

Yes!
Let us throw these stones
Let our ripples grow
Tsunami tidal waves that usher in
New days
Of community, culture, poetry and song

This is what they have feared all along

<u>BONUS TRACKS: MIC DROP MICROS</u>

*(special shout out to Jennifer Gordon Poetry
for the amazing catch phrase!)*

*I don't go around cracking open Pandora boxes
For nothing
~Julian Matthews (Can Opener)~*

Capitalism

This OG pyramid scheme
Got us all making memes
Instead of inciting revolution

Welcome to reverse evolution

Amend the 13th

Emancipation
Pardon the restoration
Feigned deliverance

Divisions Envisioned

Windows to the world
Clearly viewing limited
Seats at the table

Danger Will Robinson

It seems that everyone speaks in anger these days
We've all become fluent in rage
As we all start to drown
In communication breakdown
Lost in space in this digital age

InDoctoredNation

The climate of our social condition
Has dropped below zero
God has no reason to bless this America

Six-Word Love Story

Boy meets girl
Equation for disaster

That One Night

We should have just fucked
But we made love…

Fuck

On Second Thought

Just when you thought
The love was true
You find
They've put a spell on you

Check and Mate

Love is a game
Strategically played
Your thoughts and emotions
Openly splayed
But once you give ground
You can lose all you've found
Play cautiously else
You become self-betrayed

Current Mood

Go fuck yourself…
No safe word

Preying for Privilege

System created
One population favored
Living in loopholes

Media Circus

You should understand
It's just a fraction of the plan
These roadside distractions

#ClickBait

In the age of algorithms
Nothing is true
The data is driven
And the vehicle is you

GhostWriters

Lost correspondence
Warning Sign: Do Not Repeat
Invisible ink

The Annihilation Tango

And thusly shall I collapse
Parallel with this world
My stardust unfurled
As we danse macabre into oblivion

Another Happy Couple

In this scene together
We're seen together
But does it seem together
When these seams rip the tether
Will these screams last forever
Or these dreams escape the never
As we hide under the weather
Admit the truth never
When we're seen together
In this scene together

Two-Tone Jenny

She ghosted me again today
I should not be surprised
Previous poisonous patterns
Perpetuate pain
Once again

One heart can only hold so much blood

We Found Love

Cowering in dark corners
Trying to hide
So many inner-demons
Now residing outside

Inviting them back in
To ponder this plight
We finally made the choice to unite
To at least try to make it right

We found love

Fatherly Advice

Your bottled message
Weighs hard on my shattered bones
Comes through loud and clear

Home Is Where

I left you there
Life and breath and breaking bread
We no longer share

Flailing Daily

Not a day goes by
I don't cry out in questions
Forgotten lessons

One can only live
Within freefall for so long
Til the heart just stops

Just One Step

Poor exhausted soul
You have a hard road to climb
To find tomorrow

Homogenized Banter

Damn girl, you're so phat
The cream done rose to the top
Let's stir something up

The Silence Between

If you're just a stray
Post it in the notes not played
Jazz me poetic

Road Closed Ahead

These words between us
Navigating the distance
Since the bridge collapsed

Starving Artist

Hungry for your love
Table scraps become a feast
When given no choice

Waving the Red Flag

An empty suitcase
Longing to be filled again
Heavy with baggage

The Forest & the Trees

Suicidal thoughts
Not the escape plan I need
Thank goodness for weed
Impossible logic got you down?
Never fear, poetry is back in town

Ode to The Dark Verses

Life is suffering
We are the shadowdancers
Bridging light's music

Life and Liberty are in Pursuit

Just who is this we of which you speak
Why is this secret you need to keep
If truth be told
These threads unfold
When we shine the light on whence you creep

All About Perspective

Reality shows
Morality plays
Humanity is going
Through quite the phase
None too worried
Turtle wins the race

DarkStar

The scars on her skin
Mark the beauty
That was forced
To live within

(As of Yet) Untitled

If ink be my blood
I have a poem-sized heart
You are the title

One Night in Hartford

My watercolors
And your waterproof canvas
Temporary art

Fools Gold
(Collab with Elias Soria)

Grand expectations
Not enough to save the day
Even rainbows end

Just Another Fairytale

Once upon a time
A poet still believed in
Forever after

Breakout! _(From the Dogma Pound)_

Don't allow structured religions
To cage you in
When spirituality
Invites you to fly free

The Beltane Boogie

Jesus saw his shadow
From the cave he did emerge
Now six more years of hell on Earth
We are left to serve
But on Beltane nights
We reserve our rights
Dancing to our own rhythms
Just as we deserve

The People Dichotomy

The first word was held
In the heart of the mother
We should have listened

Preferred Perspective

Try this pronoun on
God identifies as we
Just think about it

Wounded Knee Massacred

Prayer ties, sage and sweetgrass
Littered with beer bottles, cigarette butts
And shell casings
Marking the landscape
With the venn diagram
Of the colonizers

Poetically Speaking

Why write poetry
Axe murder is illegal
The road less traveled

Direct Message

Circumlocution
This just does not work for me
I got shit to say

This Rock is Crumbling

The cornerstone
Cannot stand alone
It must have support surrounding

Final Word

Poets are like trees
Roots growing even through rocks
Life will find a way

Epilogue...or Prologue
(it's up to us to decide...)

One person gathers what another one spills.
~The Grateful Dead~

Changeling Studios is Bear Wolf
(with a little help from my friends).

With multiple personalities…oops, I mean performance personas…it just felt right to put it all in one place. Living within my continuing struggles with the human race and all its fickle fanciful contradictions that exist in the endless dichotomies of all its potential that is wholly wasted, realized and actualized all at the same time, it felt necessary to just do it all myself up to this point, no attempted submissions, no publishers, no agents, no recording contracts or tour managers, etc. Thusly Changeling Studios was created.

This journey has been an interesting one to be sure: musician, poet, writer, performer, teacher, member of multiple slam teams, nerd store owner and all-around wanderer and nomad. The one thing that I have always been best at, that has always called to me, that has been consistent in my half-century of existence in this current incarnation, is my ability to chronicle this entire human existence from a point of view that strives to get to the heart, the soul, the center, the core. I have always hoped my superpower was the ability to assist others in being the best possible versions of themselves that they can be, but alas, I think I may have been gifted instead with a sixth sense for bullshit. As a result, I have been questioning our existence since I was five or six years old.

This has *not* always served me well, in jobs, careers, interpersonal relationships, legal matters, life in general, but I truly have no choice but to keep doing it. When I have tried to keep my inner voice from breaking out, I have only succeeded in further deepening my depression and anxiety issues and giving myself repeated identity crises. The only time I ever truly feel like I am being my true self is when I'm performing and/or creating.

I sincerely hope that what I have shared with you reverberates with your own vibrations and our ripples go out into the universe to help it evolve into the greater space it can truly be. I hope that I have succeeded in making you think, laugh, cry, or at the very least, I have entertained in some way. Thank you for encouraging my behavior, for I am the epitome of a starving artist (musician/poet/writer/performer) because rhyme doesn't pay.

*Take nothing but memories
Leave nothing but footprints
~The Universe~*

www.ingramcontent.com/pod-product-compliance
Lightning Source LLC
Chambersburg PA
CBHW051454150726
48000CB00005B/2393